What's In the Name of Jesus?

Contents

What's in a Name?

In the name of Jesus, I have all that I need. In the Greek language, this word name is *onoma* and carries with it several meanings. Onoma is *character which is described by the name.* It also refers to *delegated power and authority that is associated with a name.*

A name is the substitute or representative of a person. In the Holy Bible, a person's name was not just something for identification. It was indicative of one's attributes, character, and description.

When we hear or mention a person's name, it brings to our mind the whole person: what we know of that individual; the impression that person has made on us. The mention of a name can also elicit certain emotions within us, whether good or bad.

Believers have a promise in John 14:13-14 that says, *And whatsoever ye shall ask in my name, that will I do, that the Father may be glorified in the Son. If ye shall ask any thing in my name, I will do it.* This promise means He will do what we ask as it is in alignment with His character and conformable to His purpose. He must be glorified!

Why So Many Names?

God reveals Himself to us by various names that we may witness the full manifestation of His attributes and understand the character which the name denotes. There are many names as well as titles of my Lord Jesus. It takes many names because He is so infinite and limitless. The various names and titles are how I can come to understand the all of Who He Is!

The Lord reveals to us Himself through His many names and meets the various needs in our life by those precious names. The many and diverse layers of His relationship with us is revealed in and through His names.

We are saved, healed, delivered, sustained and all our needs are supplied because of who He is. All we need, all that God has promised us is wrapped up IN THE NAME OF JESUS!

In the Name of Jesus...!

And they that know thy name will put their trust in thee: for thou, LORD, hast not forsaken them that seek thee. Psalms 9:10

To *know* indicates intimate relationship with someone. It is more than a mere acquaintance. To know someone you must spend time him/her. Engage in conversation. Understand his/her thoughts, desires, and motives. When we know the Lord, we can put our trust in Him because we believe He is true to His Word. We have spent time with Him. We understand His ways, thoughts, and motives.

This word trust in the Hebrew is *batach*. It means to *attach oneself to; to feel safe; be secure.* It basically describes a confident mind. When we are developing a right relationship with the Lord, we can dwell and live securely in Him.

As we meditate on the names of Jesus and understand all that is ours in that name, we shall develop intimacy with Him and deepen our faith in Him.

Scripture Meditations

O LORD our Lord, how excellent is thy name in all the earth! Psalms 8:9

From the rising of the sun unto the going down of the same the LORD'S name is to be praised. Psalms 113:3

The name of the LORD is a strong tower: the righteous runneth into it, and is safe. Proverbs 18:10

Wherefore God also hath highly exalted him, and given him a name which is above every name: That at the name of Jesus every knee should bow, of things in heaven, and things in earth, and things under the earth; And that every tongue should confess that Jesus Christ is Lord, to the glory of God the Father. Philippians 2:9-11

And blessed be his glorious name for ever: and let the whole earth be filled with his glory; Amen, and Amen. Psalms 72:19

Be it known unto you all, and to all the people of Israel, that by the name of Jesus Christ of Nazareth, whom ye crucified, whom God raised from the dead, even by him doth this man stand here before you whole. This is the stone which was set at nought of you builders, which is become the head of the corner. Neither is there salvation in any other: for there is none other name under heaven given among men, whereby we must be saved. Acts 4:10-12

Forasmuch as there is none like unto thee, O LORD; thou art great, and thy name is great in might. Jeremiah 10:6

Emmanuel – God with Us
Matthew 1:23

Behold, a virgin shall be with child, and shall bring forth a son, and they shall call his name Emmanuel, which being interpreted is, God with us.

Emmanuel, Son of the Living God. *'God with me.'* He is the greatest promise of God fulfilled in the earth. Not only does He dwell with me, He dwells in me by His Holy Spirit!

God's desire has always been toward His people. He has always desired fellowship with me. One of the greatest things to me is that I can know God personally and intimately.

The eternal promises of God for me were wrapped in a little baby named Emmanuel which means God with us. God gave me a blessed assurance of His eternal presence with me when His Word became flesh!

Along with His presence comes His Love, His favor, forgiveness, and the all of who He is. God became His Word with a body.

Because God is with me doesn't mean that I will have no struggles, temptations, or even failures in life. It does mean that I will have the presence of the Living God with me. I can still walk in victory in the midst of what looks like failure!

No matter what difficulties are in my life, I must see myself as being embraced and surrounded by a loving, caring, and faithful God.

Prayer:

Thank you Jesus for being Emmanuel, God with me. Every day in every situation You are with me. You are with me to love me, to guide me, to fellowship with me. Teach me to be aware of Your presence in my everyday life. In Jesus name, Amen.

Notes:

The Vine

John 15:5
I am the vine, ye are the branches: He that abideth in me, and I in him, the same bringeth forth much fruit: for without me ye can do nothing.

As a believer in the Lord Jesus Christ and having accepted Him as personal Lord and Savior, I am now in HIM. I am a branch attached to He who is the Vine. The Vine has all the resources and nutrients the branch needs in order to be sustained, matured, and bear fruit.

As I abide in the Vine, I shall grow in Christlike character and bear fruit. What fruit will I bear? The fruit of the Spirit found in Galatians 5:22-23: *But the fruit of the Spirit is love, joy, peace, longsuffering, gentleness, goodness, faith, Meekness, temperance: against such there is no law.*

The Holy Spirit flows through the Vine and into my life. As I yield to the obedience of the Holy Spirit, the fruit of the Spirit will be developed within my heart. The fruit of the Holy Spirit should always be developing in me. I should daily be maturing and growing in Christlike character. I can't make this happen on my own. Fruit cannot be forced to mature. Fruit matures when the branch is securely attached to the Vine.

My responsibility is to abide in the Vine. *How do I abide in the Vine?*

    ☐ Read the Word of God
    ☐ Study the Word of God
    ☐ Meditate the Word of God
    ☐ Practice the Presence of God

I must maintain a daily relationship with God. As I walk in obedience to His Word, the Holy Spirit will flow through me and He will mature me. The Holy Spirit produces the fruit. I will become like Jesus as I abide in He who is the Vine.

Prayer:

Thank you Father that as I abide in Your Word and walk in obedience and surrender to Your Word, You are faithful to transform my life into one that bears fruit for Your Kingdom. In Jesus name, Amen.

Notes:

The Word of Life

I John 1:1-3

That which was from the beginning, which we have heard, which we have seen with our eyes, which we have looked upon, and our hands have handled, of the Word of life; 2 (For the life was manifested, and we have seen it, and bear witness, and shew unto you that eternal life, which was with the Father, and was manifested unto us;) 3 That which we have seen and heard declare we unto you, that ye also may have fellowship with us: and truly our fellowship is with the Father, and with his Son Jesus Christ.

Here I have the revelation by John that Jesus is the Word of Life. He recounts that Jesus was in the beginning with God. With his eyes, John saw the Lord. With his ears John heard the voice of the Savior and with his hands John touched He who is the Word made flesh, the Word of Life!

His Word is eternal and gives eternal life. Not only does His Word give eternal life, it releases new life and vitality into my spirit, soul, and body. There will never be a situation in life for which God has not already provided a Word of Life for me. There is a Word for my life – now! I must prayerfully search the Scriptures for the Word that relates to my need, I must then remain focused in the Word that the Holy Spirit reveals to my spirit.

As I prayerfully search the Scriptures, I can ask the Holy Spirit to lead me and give me a word to meditate on. Meditating the Word will keep my mind on the Lord so that I won't be overcome by worry and anxiety during difficult and trying seasons. The Word is more powerful than any difficult situation in life!

The Word of Life

Prayer:

Thank You Lord for being my Word of Life. Touch my eyes that I may see as You see, touch my ears that I may hear Your voice with clarity, and touch my hands that I may reach out and touch others with your love. In Jesus name, Amen.

Notes:

He Who Is the Same

Hebrews 13:8
Jesus Christ the same yesterday, and today, and forever.

Uncertainty is everywhere. Stability is fleeting. Who knows what the stock market will be! Gas prices up and down! Shaky economy! However, the Word of God never changes!!! Since the Holy Bible is the Word of God and the Word of God are the promises of God, the promises of God do not change. The character of God does not change because of the stock market, the economy or man's indecisiveness.

As I read throughout the Bible, I see how the hand of the Lord was with His people to feed and sustain them. His power was available to fight for them. His grace and mercy always there to save them. This is my hope in times like these.

Jesus is the same in the 21$_{st}$ Century. He will feed and sustain every believer. He who is the same will deliver, set free, and answer prayer. He rains on the just and the unjust. His mercy still endures forever and all who call on Him will be saved.

I can have stability in my mind and heart when I place my confidence in He who is stable and never changes. It is His word that stabilizes me.

He will also not change His mind about sin. I must repent of it and allow Him to wash me and cleanse me from it. He does not want sin to have dominion over me. If I confess my sin, He who is the same is faithful and just to forgive me and cleanse me from all unrighteousness!

Prayer:

Lord, I thank You for being my stability in an unstable world. Your Word is faithful and True and it will never change. Teach me to depend totally on Your faithfulness to Your Word to me. In Jesus name, Amen.

Notes:

My Hope

I Timothy 1:1

Paul, an apostle of Jesus Christ by the commandment of God our Saviour, and Lord Jesus Christ, which is our hope...

Paul is writing to his son in the ministry, Timothy. He greets Timothy in the name of our Lord Jesus Christ who is our hope. This word *hope* means *desire of some good with expectation of obtaining it; trust; confidence in someone.*

Since hope is *a desire of something good with expectation of obtaining it,* my hope must remain in Jesus.

Jesus is my foundation of hope. Hope helps me to faithfully continue praying regardless of what circumstances look like. No matter what situations life presents to me, my hope is anchored in the Lord's goodness, grace, mercy, and especially His faithfulness.

Because it walks beside expectation, hope is my stabilizer. It will bring stability to my mind and emotions in times of difficulty. My hope is nourished as I read the Word expectantly. My confidence is not based on knowing that everything will turn out the way I want it to. It is rooted in believing that God loves me and is faithful to work all things together for my good!

Hope urges me to wait confidently for the salvation of the Lord. Hope in Christ gives me a strength that enables me to endure hardship as a good soldier and gives me the grace I need to be patient regardless of what I'm facing. Jesus is my Hope!

My Hope

Prayer:

Lord, my hope is in You. I wholly lean on and trust in Your name, Your strength, and Your wisdom and power. Help me to be patient and wait for You. Thank You for working all things together for my good. Some things I don't understand, however, I hope in You, Lord. Renew my Strength.   In Jesus name, Amen.

Notes:

The Rock

I Corinthians 10:1-4

Moreover, brethren, I would not that ye should be ignorant, how that all our fathers were under the cloud, and all passed through the sea; ₂ And were all baptized unto Moses in the cloud and in the sea; ₃ And did all eat the same spiritual meat; ₄ And did all drink the same spiritual drink: for they drank of that spiritual Rock that followed them: and that Rock was Christ.

A rock! Not a pebble. Not a stone. A rock epitomizes strength. This rock represents the protection, permanence, stability, and faithfulness of a loving Savior! The Rock is always with me. Rocks are known to provide shelter and safety in the wilderness in times of storms and extreme heat.

The Rock remains steadfast. His plans and purpose for me are unchanging. He is always for my good. During those times when it seems like my life is out of control, I must rely on the strength of The Rock to stabilize my mind and protect me.

His strong character and stable faithfulness provide me with the strength I need to withstand any situation that comes and threatens to disturb my peace of mind.

Whatever comes to try and shake my confidence in the promises of God for my life cannot overcome me. The foundation of my life is built on Jesus Christ, the Solid Rock. I am secure in Him and on His Word. Jesus is my Rock!

The Rock

Prayer:

Lord, You are more stable, faithful, and reliable than anything or anyone I know. When my heart is overwhelmed and I'm shaken by life's issues, You steady and stabilize me.

There is no rock like you my Lord. You are my Fortress, in You I will trust. You are my rock in whom I take refuge. Thank You Jesus. Thank You for being the strength of my life. In Jesus' name, Amen.

Notes:

The *I AM*

John 8:54-59

Jesus answered, If I honour myself, my honour is nothing: it is my Father that honoureth me; of whom ye say, that he is your God: ₅₅ *Yet ye have not known him; but I know him: and if I should say, I know him not, I shall be a liar like unto you: but I know him, and keep his saying.* ₅₆ *Your father Abraham rejoiced to see my day: and he saw it, and was glad.* ₅₇ *Then said the Jews unto him, Thou art not yet fifty years old, and hast thou seen Abraham?* ₅₈ *Jesus said unto them, Verily, verily, I say unto you, Before Abraham was, I am.*

Praise God for He who is the I AM! He is my I AM and I AM His!!!

The I AM who was in the beginning with God is God. The same I AM who told Moses in Exodus 3:14, 'And God said unto Moses, *I AM THAT I AM...*' is with me today! Thank you Jesus!

My I AM is present with me, listens for me, and answers my prayers.

I AM speaks and is slow to anger.
I AM is my Provider.
I AM is Gracious.
I AM is my Healer.
I AM is blessing me right now!
I AM is my Deliverer.
I Am is the presence of God with me!!!

The I AM

Prayer:

Thank You Jesus for being my I AM. You are all that I need. I bow before You in adoration of who You are. Thank You Lord! I glorify You and lift You up. You alone are worthy to be praised. Hallelujah! Bless Your Holy Name!

Notes:

A Savior

Matthew 1:20-21

But while he thought on these things, behold, the angel of the Lord appeared unto him in a dream, saying, Joseph, thou son of David, fear not to take unto thee Mary thy wife: for that which is conceived in her is of the Holy Ghost. [21] And she shall bring forth a son, and thou shalt call his name JESUS: for he shall save his people from their sins.

The name Jesus means *"Yahweh saves."* The word *saved* in this text is the Greek word *sozo.* Sozo means *salvation in regard to material as well as temporal deliverance from danger and suffering. It is also the spiritual and eternal salvation to those who believe in Jesus Christ.*

Sozo also includes within its context *God's power to deliver from the bondage of sin and the blessings of God which He gives to them that are in Christ.*

I realize now that when I accepted Jesus Christ as my Savior – He had me fully covered. I received full coverage insurance in Him. If I do wrong and repent, His salvation covers me with forgiveness, grace, and mercy. If someone or something else hurts me, His salvation includes healing and deliverance from the bondages of sin.

Goodness and mercy follow me. His angels are encamped around me. His Blood covers me. Underneath me are the everlasting arms. I am covered by my Savior.

A Savior

Prayer:

Thank You Jesus for covering every aspect of my life with salvation. In saving me You provide coverage for deliverance, healing and blessings. I'm covered by your precious blood. Thank You! Thank You! Thank You! I don't have to live in fear – for You have me covered! You knew that I needed a Savior before I knew it and You were here waiting for me. Thank You so much my Savior and my Lord!!! In Jesus' name, Amen

Notes:

A Helper

Hebrews 13:5-6
Let your conversation be without covetousness; and be content with such things as ye have: for he hath said, I will never leave thee, nor forsake thee. ₆ So that we may boldly say, The Lord is my helper,

and I will not fear what man shall do unto me.

The dictionary defines help as *to make things easier or better; to cause improvement in; to give assistance.* A *helper* is *one that helps*.

To have the Lord as my Helper is better than man being on my side. With the Lord as my Helper, His strength is my strength, His wisdom is my wisdom. He is my Source and Resource.

Knowing that Jesus is my Helper no matter what situation I face gives me courage to stand and be strong. Even in situations of distress, if I call on the Lord, He has promised to answer me and be with me. As my Helper, Jesus has promised to never leave me nor forsake me!

Trusting in the Lord as my Helper releases me from tormenting fears and anxieties that would overwhelm me.

Everything I need to succeed is with me. Whatever I'm lacking, I have grace which helps me! Worry can now leave and fear can be destroyed – I have Help to overcome.

Help is here to strengthen me!
Help is here to encourage me!
Help is here to sustain me!

My Helper is compassionate yet firm and gracious; slow to anger, and abounds in love and faithfulness. Day by day in every way – the Lord is my Helper! Thank You Jesus!

A Helper

Prayer:

Thank You Jesus for being my Helper. I am grateful that You have promised to never leave me nor forsake me.

Forgive me for the times when I didn't trust You and relied on my own understanding, strength, intellect, and friends. There is none like You. You alone are mighty to save. Thank You! In Jesus' name, Amen.

Notes:

The Good Shepherd

John 10:11
*I am the good shepherd: the good shepherd giveth his life for the
sheep.*

A Good Shepherd is One who protects, cares for, nurtures, and feeds the sheep. His primary concern is for the welfare of the sheep. He provides protection from predators and anything that would seek to devour and destroy His sheep.

Sheep are prone to wander off from the sheepfold and from the protective care of the Shepherd. Imagine that! When sheep are afraid, they become paralyzed which leaves them vulnerable to the enemy. Sometimes they are even to afraid to *'baaa'* for help!

The Lord Jesus is my Shepherd. He alone is my Good Shepherd! Like sheep, I have at times gone astray. I have fallen prey to the wiles of the enemy and become vulnerable to the troubles and cares of the world.

I must be His sheep because Jesus said *"My sheep hear my voice.'* Times when I have been afraid and vulnerable to the enemy, I hear my Good Shepherd whispering a Scripture in my spirit. He will bring a Word of encouragement to my mind or a song to my heart.

The Good Shepherd does this in order to draw me to Himself and away from the cares and distractions of the world. These things would have destroyed me had I not listened to and obeyed the voice of my Good Shepherd!

The Good Shepherd has given His life for me so that I can live eternally with Him.

The Good Shepherd

Prayer:

Heavenly Father, thank You for being my Good Shepherd. You so loved me that You gave Your only begotten Son, that if I believe on Him, I shall not perish, but have everlasting life. You alone redeemed me from the hand of the enemy. While I was yet a sinner, You died for me. You protect me, nourish me, lead and guide me. Help me to follow You always. Thank You for watching over me day and night. In Jesus' name, Amen.

Notes:

A Hen

Matthew 23:37

O Jerusalem, Jerusalem, thou that killest the prophets, and stonest them which are sent unto thee, how often would I have gathered thy children together, even as a hen gathereth her chickens under her wings, and ye would not!

A hen portrays the protecting, loving, nurturing, and continuous care that God gives me. In this scripture Jerusalem refused what the Lord Jesus was providing them as a hen. Unlike them, I desire all that He provides for me. Lord, I want to live under the protective care of Your wings!

The Lord Jesus is as a mother hen that provides warmth, refuge, and security from the adversary. The adversary of my soul goes about as a roaring lion seeking whom he may devour. Jesus is my mother Hen. He will cover me.

When I stand for what God calls right, He covers me. Even though others may call right wrong and wrong right, God covers me when I do what is right. He covers me so that insults from others cannot penetrate into my spirit. His Word covers my soul.

My safety is under His wings. Psalms 91:14 reminds me that *He shall cover me with his feathers and under His wings I take refuge.*

A Hen

Prayer:
Thank You for being my refuge and my safety. My soul trusts in You. In the shadow of Your wings I hide. In Jesus' name, Amen.

Notes:

The Bread of Life

John 6:48 – 51

I am that bread of life. 49 Your fathers did eat manna in the wilderness, and are dead. 50 This is the bread which cometh down from heaven, that a man may eat thereof, and not die. 51 I am the living bread which came down from heaven: if any man eat of this bread, he shall live for ever: and the bread that I will give is my flesh, which I will give for the life of the world

Bread has always been known as the staple of life because it gives so much nourishment to the body. There is nothing that smells as good as freshly baked homemade bread! It can be a pretty golden brown with butter melting on the top. As it sits on a pretty plate on the table, I can choose what to do with it. I can share it with others or just sit and admire it. I can dream about its taste and texture or I can put it in the cupboard and save it. This does nothing for me inwardly. I must sit down, slice the bread, and eat it myself!

So it is with the Bread of Life! It is not enough to look at my Bible or even think about a few verses every now and then. I must open the Bible and feed on the Word of God. There must be a daily ingestion and digestion of the Bread of Life into my heart and life.

I can only be strengthened and nourished in my spiritual life and walk with the Lord by spending time eating the Word and applying it to my life. The nutrients of the Word sustain me and keep me from becoming weak in faith.

I refuse to feast on doubt and unbelief by listening to the whispers of the enemy. With childlike faith I sit at the table of the Lord and feast on His Word. My soul must be nourished by the Living Bread of healing, salvation, and wholeness.

The Bread of Life

Prayer:

Lord, Your Word is my Bread of Life. Guide me by Your Holy Spirit so that I may understand Your Word. Thank You that as I take in the Bread of Life and purpose to live by it, You will strengthen, sustain, and revive me. In Jesus' name, Amen.

Notes:

The Author and Finisher of My Faith

Hebrews 12:2

Looking unto Jesus the author and finisher of our faith; who for the joy that was set before him endured the cross, despising the shame, and is set down at the right hand of the throne of God.

This word *author* is a compound word. It is made up of two words; *ago*, which *means "to lead,"* and *arch, "the first."* As a compound word it means *"the chief leader; one who takes the lead and furnishes the example."*

The word *finisher* in the Greek means a *completer, perfecter; one who brings something through to the goal so as to win and receive the prize.*

This scripture describes Jesus as the One who surpasses the examples of faith in Hebrews 11. Jesus is the Giver, the Originator, and the example of my faith. He also serves as my mentor in the faith. As the Source and the Author of my faith, Romans 12:3 reminds me that Jesus has already given me a measure of faith. I must use it! Not only has He given me the capacity for faith, He has provided Himself as the object of my faith! He will bring me through to the intended goal. He that hath begun a good work in me shall complete it.

As I continue to look to Jesus and walk by the faith He has given me, His promises and purpose for my life will be fulfilled. Jesus Christ is in me by His Spirit. I must stay focused on the indwelling Christ. As I believe and walk in His Word, His Word in me combines with the faith that is in me and gives me wisdom to be more than a conqueror.

The Author and Finisher of My Faith

Prayer:
   Thank You Lord for giving me faith and for being the object of my faith. You are my example and my mentor. When I feel weak in faith I will still trust in Your Word.

Notes:

The Redeemer

Galatians 3:13

Christ hath redeemed us from the curse of the law, being made a curse for us: for it is written, Cursed is every one that hangeth on a tree:

To *redeem* means *to buy back; to recover.* It refers to the purchasing of slaves or hostages for the purpose of setting them free.

In biblical terms, redemption is *the act by which God delivered me from the bondage of sin by the sacrifice of Jesus Christ.*

I have been redeemed by the blood of the Lamb. Jesus has paid the price for me with His own blood so that I don't have to be controlled and enslaved to sin by the enemy.

Jesus, my Redeemer has set me free. I belong to Him. My body belongs to the Lord. Thanks be to God, I have been rescued from the hand of the enemy. My Redeemer sent His Word to heal and deliver me from destructions.

Because Jesus is my Redeemer, I don't have to be entangled with the yoke of bondage. I am free from the dominion of sin. Christ does not want me to live under the curse of the law so He became a curse for me to take the curse from me. Thank You Jesus!

In Revelation 5:9, it is the redeemed that are praising the Lamb of God for He has redeemed us to God by His blood. Every nation is represented. Every language and nationality has been redeemed. Everyone will be united in one Spirit of love before the throne of God. I will worship the Lord along with my brothers and sisters in Christ from every nation and language. Hallelujah!

I have been bought with a great price. Lord, with all that is within me, I will glorify You! I will bless Your holy and righteous name. The enemy cannot have a hold on me because I belong to God. I will walk and live in the freedom that is mine in Jesus Christ. I will rejoice in the Lord.

The Redeemer

Prayer:

My Savior and my Lord!

You alone have redeemed me from every curse and from the hand of the enemy. Thank You for shedding Your blood for me. I am so grateful for Your great sacrifice. You didn't have to do it but You did. Thank You Jesus! Thank You Jesus! Thank You Jesus!

How can I serve You better, Lord? Teach me. I will walk in Your ways. I desire to walk in obedience to You. I surrender all to You! Thank You!!! I Love You, Lord! In Jesus' name, Amen.

Notes:

The Lord of All

Acts 10:36-37
*The word which God sent unto the children of Israel, preaching
peace by Jesus Christ: (he is Lord of all*

All means everything. I can't hold back on God by allowing Him
to reign in my life on Sundays then do whatever I want to do
Monday through Saturday. He must have all of me all the time. The
Lord will not fight me to be my Lord. He will not force me to make
Him Lord of all my life. He has graciously given me that choice. In
the Old Testament, God would tell His children *'I have set before
you life and death – choose life.'* He gives us a choice and tells us
what the best choice is. Life is always the best choice. Since He is
life, He is the best and the right choice. I can choose the Lord to rule
as Lord of all my life, or I can choose myself. I can even choose
someone or something else to rule my life.

How often I go to Church or even how often I talk about the Lord
is not the basis of my Christian life. Jesus Christ must be The Lord
of All of my life. His ways must rule in my heart, my soul, life,
conduct, and conversation. I must allow Him to govern my words
and His ways must govern my lifestyle.

I must trust Him enough to make decisions based on *"not my will,
but Thy will be done"* in my life. Only when I have yielded to His
word through obedience can I see God's Divine purpose unfold in
my life.

Obedient surrender to His will and to His revealed word in my life
makes this possible. I choose Jesus to be the Lord of all my life.
Daily! I'm learning to let go of other things and even people who
would control me. I want Jesus to be my Lord. I choose to be
governed by his Word and His ways.

Prayer:

Lord Jesus, You are the Lord of all of me!!! Fill me with Your Holy Spirit. I give myself to You so that You can use me. Fulfill Your Divine Purpose in and through me. Have your way in my life. Be Lord of all there is in my life. In Jesus' name, Amen.

Notes:

Him Who Called Me Out of Darkness

I Peter 2:9
But ye are a chosen generation, a royal priesthood, an holy nation, a peculiar people; that ye should shew forth the praises of him who hath called you out of darkness into his marvellous light:

Often I pray Psalms 119:*18* which says *Open thou mine eyes, that I may behold wondrous things out of Thy law.* The Hebrew word for *open* is *galah* and means His Light I begin to see all that God has done and is doing. It is amazing. I don't want to walk in darkness. I miss out on the wondrous things God has and Is.

When in darkness, there is depression, discouragement, and much dismay. The enemy of my soul tries to keep me in darkness so I won't come to the realization of Who God is and who I am in Him. Now that I am walking in the Light of the Lord's understanding, I realize that He has chosen me. He has made me royalty in Him. I am holy because He is holy and He dwells in me. I am peculiar!!!

This is reason to praise Him. I don't have to walk in darkness. Anytime I do not have an answer or need to understand something, I can go to God in prayer. He is still bringing me out of the darkness of ignorance and giving me His wisdom.

Him Who Called Me Out of Darkness

Prayer:
Lord, make Your Word power and Light in my heart. Thank You for calling me out of darkness that I may walk in Your Light of understanding. Open my eyes that I may continue to behold wondrous things in Your Word and in my life. I will show forth Your praise. In Jesus' name, Amen.

Notes:

The Fourth Man in the Fire

Daniel 3:21-25

Then these men were bound in their coats, their hosen, and their hats, and their other garments, and were cast into the midst of the burning fiery furnace. 22 Therefore because the king's commandment was urgent, and the furnace exceeding hot, the flame of the fire slew those men that took up Shadrach, Meshach, and Abednego. 23 And these three men, Shadrach, Meshach, and Abednego, fell down bound into the midst of the burning fiery furnace. 24 Then Nebuchadnezzar the king was astonied , rose up in haste, and spake, and said unto his counsellors, Did not we cast three men bound into the midst of the fire? They answered and said unto the king, True, O king. 25 He answered and said, Lo, I see four men loose, walking in the midst of the fire, and they have no hurt; and the form of the fourth is like the Son of God

Daniel Chapter 3 tells tells me how these young men refused to bow and were condemned to death by being thrown into a fiery furnace. They trusted in the Lord God and remained true to Him. After being thrown into the fiery furnace, the preincarnate Jesus Christ joined them in the fire!

Being a witness for the Lord will sometimes get me in hot water – or the lion's den! I must not be ashamed of His word or His ways. If I'm ashamed of Him, I will deny Him. If I deny Him, He will deny me before the Father. In actuality, if I deny Him, I'm denying myself of His power to save me and destroy my adversaries.

In the midst of standing up for God, Jesus stood up for them. He stepped from His throne in glory into the fire and flames of persecution, took the heat out of the flame, and it became a time of fellowship and communion.

When I walk in the light of God's Word and take a stand for Him, He will stand with me and for me. Jesus is with me in every difficult situation I face.

The Fourth Man

Prayer:

Almighty God, help every believer to be strong in You and in the power of Your might!

When I stand on Your Word, it often goes against the views of society. Thank You for being with me in the midst of every difficult situation. The world is calling right wrong and wrong right. What You call sin is becoming acceptable behavior. I will trust in Your Word and stand strong knowing that You are with me! In Jesus' name, Amen.

Notes:

The Overseer of My Soul

I Peter 2:25

*For ye were as sheep going astray; but are now returned unto the
Shepherd and Bishop of your souls.*

The Greek word for overseer is *episkopos*. It means *"to oversee; to
watch over."* An overseer is *someone who watches over you for your
good. An overseer also has authority over the one watched.*
As the overseer of my soul, Jesus oversees and is concerned about
every detail of my life. If it concerns me, it concerns the Overseer of
my soul. Jesus watches over my life and guides me by His Spirit. He
desires that I abide under His authority. My soul contains my mind,
my will, and my emotions. My Overseer watches over my mind with
his Word. He will keep my emotions balanced. He desires that my
will be consumed by His.
He desires to have my worries as well as my worship; my
problems as well as my praise. The Lord does not want me to live in
a mindset of distress and fear.
There have been times when instead of exercising my faith, I gave
in to fear. This is how I go astray, by giving in to fear. When I focus
on the problem and my lack of resources, I am going astray from the
Overseer of my soul. Worry and anxiety cause me to go astray from
trusting in the Word of my Overseer.
I return to him in faith believing He will oversee each situation in
my life. I have tried to oversee things in my life. If I don't seek the
Lord's guidance and wisdom through prayer, my efforts are usually
futile – and I have a tendency to make some situations worse. I'm
striving to trust the Overseer of my soul in everything.

The Overseer of My Soul

Prayer:
Father, thank You for watching over me. You alone are concerned about every detail of my life; spirit, soul, and body.

Forgive me for the times I've gone astray from depending on You; from believing in Your presence with me.

There were times when my heart was so overwhelmed with hurt and disappointment, I didn't think any cared – not even You. Thank You for always having Your arms open to receive me and embrace me with Your lovingkindness. Thank You for Your grace and Your mercy toward me as the Overseer of my soul. In Jesus name, Amen.

Notes:

The Father

John 10:30
I and my Father are one.

My heavenly Father. Tender and compassionate, yet very strong and mighty. My Provider and Protector. While earthly fathers may fall short of exemplifying all that the heavenly Father is, remember, the earthly father is not the yardstick to govern God by. God cannot be held hostage because of earthly paternal examples.

God cannot be judged because of the actions of a father, mother, sister, brother, friend, or foe. All have sinned and come short of God's glory. My heavenly Father is the One who embraces me when I fall short or when I'm disappointed and discouraged because others have fallen short.

I have been created in my heavenly Father's image and can have fellowship with Him. He is never too busy for me. I can safely give my heart, love, and life to His purposes for me. As He embraces me, my cares, worries, and concerns become absorbed in His loving presence.

My fellowship with my heavenly Father is hindered if I keep my heart and mind closed to Him and focused on other things. If I start thinking that God doesn't care because other people don't seem to care, I will rob myself of the joy that He has promised me. I must remember that my heavenly Father is devoted to my salvation, my well being, and wholeness in my life. He loves me unconditionally!!!

The Father

Prayer:

Thank You for Your faithful Fatherly love, protection, and strength. I am secure in you. I am so grateful that You have called me to be Your child, Thank You, Jesus! Teach me and help me to show forth Your character in all I do. In Jesus' name, Amen.

Notes:

The Word Made Flesh

John 1:1, 14
In the beginning was the Word, and the Word was with God, and the Word was God. 14 And the Word was made flesh, and dwelt among us, (and we beheld his glory, the glory as of the only begotten of the Father,) full of grace and truth.

God gave His Holy Word a human body. Jesus is the revelation of who God is. All the promises of God were made flesh and named Jesus.

He is healing with a body. Reaching out, touching, and transforming lives. The power of His promises are so radiant, they heal all who touch Him. He is salvation - with a body to all who will believe.

When Jesus walked on the earth the promises of God were manifested in and through Him. Yes, the enemy opposed Him, however, Jesus, the Word made flesh had victory over the enemy.

Now, as a disciple of Jesus Christ, He lives within me by His Holy Spirit. As I give His Word priority in my life His Word becomes flesh within me. Christ within me reaches out to others to bring healing. The Word in me releases a word of encouragement, salvation, deliverance, and comfort to others.

Only as I'm in communion and fellowship with the Lord will His Word become flesh within me. Then I'll be the hands God uses to heal and the heart God uses to love others.

The Word Made Flesh

Prayer:
Lord Jesus, In yield to You. Let your Word become flesh within me that others may see You in me. In Jesus' name, Amen.

Notes:

The Light of the World

John 8:12

Then spake Jesus again unto them, saying, I am the light of the world: he that followeth me shall not walk in darkness, but shall have the light of life.

Jesus is the Light that shines so intensely, He vanquishes the darkness brought on by sin. This is a spiritual darkness that would lead me to eternal death. Jesus has called me from eternal death and separation from Him by His death, burial, and resurrection.

The darkness in my life can be extinguished by His Light! When the challenges in life bring darkness to the point that I can't see which way to go or don't understand '*Why*,' I must pray and seek the Light that is found in the Word of God. There is a word that will bring understanding and clarity to my life.

In the book of Genesis there was darkness upon the face of the earth. God spoke *"Let there be light"* and light broke through the vast darkness. His Word still breaks through the darkness today! There is so much power in His Word. Darkness cannot overcome His Light!

The enemy disguises himself as an angel of light, however he is the opposite of light – the prince of darkness.

As I read the Word of God, obey it, and walk in it daily, His Light becomes brighter in my spirit.

The world is becoming spiritually darker. To avoid being pulled into this darkness, I must daily pull away from the world and in prayer seek the Light. To be continually kindled by Jesus the Light of the world, there must be continuous fellowship with Him.

The Light of the World

Prayer:

Lord, be the Light in my life! The places in my life where I need the Light of understanding – teach me Your Word. Shine in and through me so that others can see You in me. In Jesus' name, Amen

Notes:

The Holy One

Acts 3:14-15
But ye denied the Holy One and the Just, and desired a murderer to be granted unto you; And killed the Prince of life, whom God hath raised from the dead; whereof we are witnesses.

Just a few days after the ascension of Jesus Christ, Peter spoke these words to the leaders of Jerusalem. He quoted an Old Testament Messianic name for Jesus Christ to them which is found in Psalms 16:10. Holy One!

In the Greek, this word *holy* is *hagios*. Its fundamental ideas are *separation, consecration, devotion to God. It is sharing in God's purity and abstaining from the defilements of the world.* Holiness speaks of the essence of the character of God. It is not one of His attributes, holiness is the totality of His being.

He who is holy has said *'Be ye holy for I am holy.'* The Lord would not have given this command had He not made provision for me to be holy as He is.

In order for me to be like Christ, I must have a relationship with Him. Otherwise, I'll just perform and have behavior that looks holy on the outside. Holiness is an inward work that is wrought by the Holy Spirit. It stems from my relationship with Jesus Christ. I have the Holy One dwelling within me and He desires to live through me to reach a dark and dying world.

The Holy One

Prayer:

Lord, as a disciple of Jesus Christ, You have called me to be holy even as You are holy. I am in the world and not of it. Help me to live and be holy as You are. I yield my heart, my thoughts, and my body to You. Holy Spirit, reveal to me the attitudes, the beliefs in my life that are contrary to Your Word. I yield to You. Make the necessary changes in me so that I may live according to Your way of holiness and righteousness.   In Jesus' name, Amen.

Notes:

My First Love

Revelation 2:4
Nevertheless I have somewhat against thee, because thou hast left thy first love.

My First Love! Jesus! He is not my first love because He's the first one that I loved. Jesus is my first love because I know that He's the first One who truly loves me.

I realize now that He loved me when I didn't even know Him. I didn't know who He was. Yes, while I was a sinner, in fact, before I was born He loved me enough to give His life for me making salvation, wholeness, healing, and deliverance possible for me.

Even after I accepted Jesus as my Savior, the lure of the world sometimes became intoxicating. At times I turned away from my First Love to see what the world had to offer. Not realizing then what I know now – that my First Love is married to the backslider! His love won't fail. He does not have love – HE IS LOVE!!!

After the intoxications of the world left me emotionally bankrupt, depleted and kicked to the curb – my First Love embraced and lifted me up. Love lifted me. My First Love wiped my tears, washed and cleansed me, seated me in heavenly places and still called me His Beloved.

Jesus is my First Love.

My First Love guides me, determines the standards for my life and convicts me when I'm wrong. I don't wander away from Him easily like I used to. If I start turning away His love and His Word draws me to Him.

You never forget your First Love!

My First Love

Prayer:

Thank You Lord for being my First Love! You loved me when I was unloveable. You sacrificed Your life for me. Thank You for loving me! In Jesus' name, Amen.

Notes:

The Lamb of God

John 1:29

The next day John seeth Jesus coming unto him, and saith, Behold the Lamb of God, which taketh away the sin of the world.

Jesus is the fulfillment of all the sacrificial systems in the Jewish tradition. He is the ultimate sacrifice for my sin. The blood of the Lamb of God washes me and cleanses me from all unrighteousness. This is how I stand complete in Him!

The salvation of my soul is secure because of the blood of the Lamb. He has taken away my sin and thrown them into the sea of forgetfulness. I am forgiven because of the blood of the Lamb.

The enemy of my soul will try to remind me of wrong things I've done and the sin I lived in, however, God has forgiven me and washed me. Thank God for the Lamb of God.

He is the precious Lamb of God who was slain for me. Because of this, He has freed me from the power of sin and death and enables me to live a life that is pleasing to God.

In gentleness and meekness the Lamb of God came into the world. In gentleness and meekness He gave His life for me.

True submission to the will of God is manifested in gentleness and meekness. Humble obedience not willful pride is what God desires from me.

The Lamb of God

Prayer:

Thank you God for the precious Lamb of God who has taken away my sin. You have forgiven me, cleansed me, washed me, and redeemed me from the hand of the enemy. Holy Spirit, breathe into my heart the Divine gentleness and meekness of the Lamb of God. Let the Fruit of You, Holy Spirit reign in my spirit. Remove pride, selfishness, and fear Thank You! Thank You! Thank You! In Jesus' name, Amen.

Notes:

The Serpent in the Wilderness

John 3:14-15
And as Moses lifted up the serpent in the wilderness, even so must the Son of man be lifted up: [15] That whosoever believeth in him should not perish, but have eternal life. For God so loved the world, that he gave his only begotten Son, that whosoever believeth in him should not perish, but have everlasting life.

In John 3, Jesus tells Nicodemus that He is the fulfillment of this type in Numbers 21:1-9. The children of Israel were in the wilderness murmuring against Moses. They complained that they had no water and no good food to eat. In the midst of their murmuring God sent fiery serpents to bite them. Moses prayed to God about their situation. The Lord told Moses to make a bronze serpent and lift it high upon a pole. Anyone who was bitten could look up at this bronze serpent and live.

The serpent was a symbol of sin and Jesus became sin for me on the cross that I can be free from sin. Just as the raised bronze serpent was the only healing remedy that God gave for the children of Israel, Jesus is the only healing remedy that God has provided for me.

The venomous serpent called sin has bitten everyone. A murmuring and complaining heart indicates a heart that is not trusting God. A heart that is not trusting God is not faithful to the Word and ways of God.

As I look up to Jesus in faith, focus on His Word, and walk in obedience, I can be healed. My emotions can be healed. The wounded places in my heart can be healed. He who knew no sin became sin for me. Galatians tells me *'Cursed is everyone that hangeth on a tree.'* I am not cursed. Jesus took my sin upon Him and took away the curse from my life. His healing virtue flows to and through me as I look to Him!

Prayer:

Father, You have provided Yourself, through Your Son, as my healer. Thank You. I glorify Your name1 You became sin for me. You took my place. Thank You!

I look to You for my complete healing. Heal the broken and wounded places in my heart and my life. Thank You for giving me eternal life in you. In Jesus' name, Amen.

Notes:

The Carpenter

Mark 6:3
*Is not this the carpenter, the son of Mary, the brother of James, and
Joses, and of Juda, and Simon? and are not his sisters here with us?
And they were offended at him.*

Jesus is the builder of my life. That which has been torn down and
ruined because of sin, wrong decisions, or a lack of wisdom, the
Carpenter can repair. He built a ladder called Calvary for me to enter
into eternal life with Him.

Matthew 16:18 reminds me that He built His Church. Have I
mistaken a building made of brick and mortar for His Church? The
Church is His people. I am just a living stone. It's me. The Carpenter
is building me. I am God's building! I Corinthians 3:9 *says For we
are labourers together with God: ye are God's husbandry, ye are
God's building.*

The Carpenter is able to sand out and smooth the rough places in
my life. He is the One who can clean up the dirty mess and
straighten things out in me. He has begun a good work in building
and rebuilding me. He will complete me.

As I trust Him, he will build up and restore the broken down places
in my life. The word of the Carpenter can dismantle and get rid of
the debris of wrong thinking patterns which have caused destruction
in my life. The Carpenter can then build up and transform my life by
the power of His Word.

The Carpenter

Prayer:
Lord Jesus, you are the Carpenter of my life. Build up what has been torn down. Smooth out my rough edges and make the crooked places straight. Renew my spirit and my mind that I may wholly live according to Your will. In Jesus' name, Amen.

Notes:

Peace

John 14:27
Peace I leave with you. My peace I give. Let not your heart be troubled…

In the Greek, this word *Peace* means *a state of untroubled, undisturbed well-being.*

Because of Jesus, I can have peace within my soul when there is turmoil all around me. So much of the world is full of strife, unrest, and distress. There are wars and rumors of wars. In the midst of it all, I can live in and experience His peace.

Brought about by God's mercy, Jesus gives me peace because of His finished work on Calvary. He grants me deliverance from the distresses that are experienced as a result of sin.

Leviticus 3:1 tells us of one of the sacrifices in the Old Testament which was a peace offering. For this offering, the animal was to be killed and its blood sprinkled on the altar. The fat of the animal was to be burned and the worshiper was to eat and enjoy its meat. Leviticus 17 lets me know that when an Israelite killed an animal for food, it was to be considered a Peace Offering and it was a time to celebrate!

Jesus is my Peace Offering! I can celebrate because of the Lamb that was slain for me. On Calvary Jesus purchased my peace. Not only did He give me peace, Ephesians 2:14 declares that *He is my Peace.*

Thanks be to God. Jesus is my Peace. I don't have to live in fear and distress. My mind does not have to be consumed with tormenting thoughts. Isaiah 26:3 reminds me that if I keep my mind on Him, *He will keep me in perfect peace.* I can have peace in my spirit, soul, and my physical body!

Peace

Prayer:

Thank You Jesus for being my Peace. You are my Peace in a troubled world. You calm and still my soul when storms are raging in my life. I trust You Lord. Thank You for loving me. In Jesus' name, Amen.

Notes:

The Burnt Offering

Hebrews 10:6-10

In burnt offerings and sacrifices for sin thou hast had no pleasure. Then said I, Lo, I come (in the volume of the book it is written of me,) to do thy will, O God. Above when he said, Sacrifice and offering and burnt offerings and offering for sin thou wouldest not, neither hadst pleasure therein; which are offered by the law; Then said he, Lo, I come to do thy will, O God. He taketh away the first, that he may establish the second. By the which will we are sanctified through the offering of the body of Jesus Christ once for all.

An animal sacrifice. Totally consumed in the flames of fire! The priest was to burn the animal on the altar. Nothing was to be left. Nothing was to be eaten as food. Totally consumed at the altar! No flesh was to be left of this animal sacrifice. The Burnt Offering in Leviticus pointed prophetically to the offering of the Lamb of God on Calvary's cross.

The Lord Jesus offered Himself totally as a sacrifice. He who knew no sin became sin by taking upon Him the sins of the world and yes, mine are included. The altar represents the Cross. The consuming flames represent the judicial wrath of God! Jesus laid on the altar for me. He was a willing sacrifice who gave His last for me. Totally until sin was consumed!

He calls me to offer myself totally to Him as a living sacrifice. He gave Himself fully for me. I can give myself fully to Him. The highest and truest worship I can give the Lord is to offer myself as a living sacrifice. I must put my entire self on the altar. Galatians 5:20 reminds me, *I am crucified with Christ: nevertheless I live; yet not I, but Christ liveth in me: and the life which I now live in the flesh I live by the faith of the Son of God, who loved me, and gave himself for me.*

The Burnt Offering

Prayer:

Thank You Jesus for being my burnt offering! I give myself to You as a living sacrifice. I put my desires and my ways on the altar. In Jesus' name, Amen.

Notes:

The Resurrection and the Life

John 11:25-26
Jesus said unto her, I am the resurrection, and the life: he that believeth in me, though he were dead, yet shall he live: And whosoever liveth and believeth in me shall never die. Believest thou this?

Resurrection means *a standing on the feet again; a rising of the body from the grave.*

Although it happened over two thousand years ago, the resurrection of Jesus Christ still impacts my life today. Because of His resurrection, I can experience resurrection in my daily walk with my risen Savior. The same resurrection power that raised Jesus from the dead and seated Him at the right hand of the Father, then put Him over all powers and principalities is the same power that has been given to me.

This is powerful. I must meditate on this until my soul is saturated with it. Jesus Christ has given me the ability to function in the realm of His resurrection power.

The cross put my old life to death. The resurrection brings me new life in Christ. The Holy Spirit within gives me oneness with Christ and equips me to do the will of God.

To access this resurrection in my life, I must die to sin and self. His power is not possible without the sacrifice of all there is in me that is of sin and selfishness. Through death there is new life. As I die to self, Christ's death works in and through me. I must daily yield myself to prayer and obedience to the Word of the Lord. This is how His resurrection power can live through me and raise me up from a dead place in my life.

Jesus passed through death so He could rise and give me new life to the glory of God.

Prayer:

Heavenly Father, I desire to experience and walk in Your resurrection power in my daily life. Reveal your truth to me and set me free from what hinders me from experiencing new life in Christ. In Jesus' name, Amen

Notes:

The Amen

Revelation 3:14
And unto the angel of the church of the Laodiceans write; These things saith the Amen, the faithful and true witness, the beginning of the creation of God;

Amen means *to make firm; to affirm; so be it; it is so.* It also conveys the idea of propping up or supporting.

The first four words of the Holy Bible are '*In the beginning God...*' the last word of the Bible is *Amen*!

When I use Amen at the close of my prayers or as a verbal exclamation of the proclaimed Word of God, it testifies to the Truth of what has been said. Being the last word in the Bible, Amen makes firm everything throughout the Bible!

Jesus confirms, supports, and upholds the Word of His Truth. He is Truth. His words will not fail. He is my eternal Amen. He alone is my eternal Truth to stand firmly on and reliably trust in.

Because Jesus is the Amen at the end of the Bible, it is Him saying, *'I Am Jesus and I AM this message!'*

The Amen

Prayer:
Father, I trust Your Word. AMEN!

Notes:

How to become a Christian

1. Realize that you are a sinner and eternally lost with Jesus Christ as you Savior.
2. Believe the good news of John 3:16-17: *For God so loved the world, that he gave his only begotten Son, that whosoever believeth in him should not perish, but have everlasting life. [17] For God sent not his Son into the world to condemn the world; but that the world through him might be saved.*
3. Believe the Jesus was born of the virgin Mary, was crucified, died, and resurrected and is alive forever to be your Advocate before God.
4. In prayer confess that you are a sinner and ask God to forgive you of your sins. John 10:9-10 tells us: *That if thou shalt confess with thy mouth the Lord Jesus, and shalt believe in thine heart that God hath raised him from the dead, thou shalt be saved. [10] For with the heart man believeth unto righteousness; and with the mouth confession is made unto salvation.*
5. *Rely on the promises of God not your feelings. Declare and believe that you are saved by faith in the blood of Jesus Christ.*

Notes

Notes

Notes

Other Books by Patty Harris

Comforting Those Who Grieve
Conquering Holiday Grief
Fear Nots for Everyday
Praying in the Key of 'C'
Restoring the Gates of Prayer
Surviving the Death of A Loved One
The T.A.S.K.S. of the Pray-er
The TRUTH About Strongholds
Thy Face, Lord, Will I Seek
What's In The Name of Jesus?
What You Can't Lose in the Midst of Loss